Write the word stop to complete the sentence.

_____

I always _____ and look both ways.

Color the stop signs red.
How many did you find? _____

This or That

Say the word. Then write the word.

that _____

Write the word **that** to complete the sentence.

_____

What is _____ ?

Color the flowers that say **this**.

How many did you find? _____

Up, Up, and Away

Say the word. Then write the word.

up _____

Write the word **up** to complete the sentence.

_____

Help me rake _____ the leaves.

Color the leaves that say **up**.

When, Where, and Why _____

Say the word. Then write the word.

when _____

Write the word **when** to complete the sentence.

I use this _____ it rains.

Beginning Sounds

Say the word for each picture.
Write the beginning sound.
Use these letters: **k, t, l, b, q, d**.

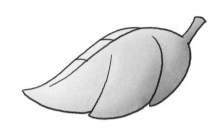

1. _____ eaf

_____ ie

2. _____ ueen

_____ og

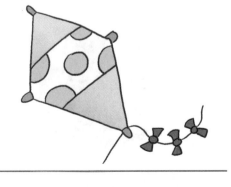

3. _____ ite

_____ all

Beginning Sounds

Say the word for each picture.
Write the beginning sound.
Use these letters: **n, y, s, g, z, j**.

1. _____ oat

_____ arn

2. _____ ine

_____ et

3. _____ oap

_____ ero

Ending Sounds

Say the word for each picture.
Write the ending sound.
Use these letters: **b, g, l, n, p, x**.

1.

pi___

cu___

2.

we___

ow___

3.

su___

fo___

Ending Sounds

Say the word for each picture.
Write the ending sound.
Use these letters: **m, k, d, l, f, r.**

1.  dru___   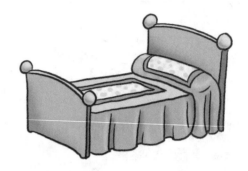 be___

2.  bea___    sea___

3.  boo___   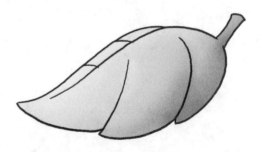 lea___

Ending Sounds

Say the word for each picture.
Write the ending sound.
Use these letters: **t, o, w, s, g, d**.

1. ca_____ co_____

2. bu_____ do_____

3. zer_____ bir_____

Beginning and Ending Sounds

Say the word for each picture.
Write the beginning and ending sounds.
Use these letters: **m**, **n**, **p**, **s**, **g**, **t**, **b**, **y**.

1. ____ o ____   ____ a ____

2. ____ e ____   ____ u ____

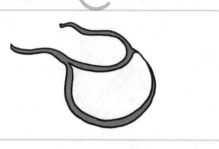 

3. ____ i ____   ____ a ____

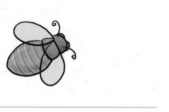 

4. ____ u ____   ____ e ____

Make a Word

Add a letter to make a new word.
Say the word.

1. _____ **all**

_____ **all**

_____ **all**

2. _____ **at**

_____ **at**

_____ **at**

3. _____ **in**

_____ **in**

_____ **in**

4. _____ **an**

_____ **an**

_____ **an**

5. _____ **et**

_____ **et**

_____ **et**

6. _____ **ell**

_____ **ell**

_____ **ell**

7. _____ **en**

_____ **en**

_____ **en**

8. _____ **ay**

_____ **ay**

_____ **ay**

9. _____ **ook**

_____ **ook**

_____ **ook**

For Your Eyes Only

Follow the directions.
Then read the message.

Color the **Z** boxes **red**.
Color the **B** boxes blue.
Color the **K** boxes green.
Color the **P** boxes yellow.

K	H	O	W	Z	B	M	A	N	Y
P	Z	M	O	N	T	H	S	K	B
A	R	E	Z	P	B	K	I	N	Z
P	B	A	K	Z	Y	E	A	R	?

Answer the question.

_____

- - - - - - - - - - - - -

_____

Colorful Shapes

Color all the triangles **green**.
Color all the circles **yellow**.
Color all the squares **red**.
Color all the rectangles **blue**.

Picture Dictionary

Circle

Square

Rectangle

Triangle

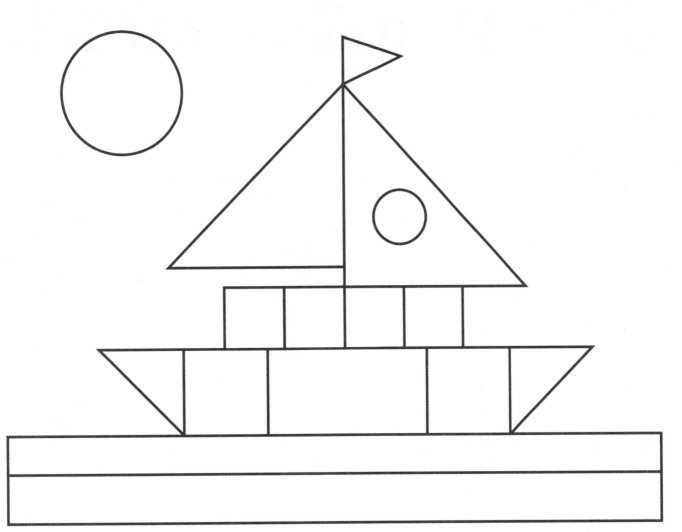

Color and Shape Words 75

Order, Please

Write **1** by what happens first.
Write **2** by what happens next.
Write **3** by what happens last.

_____ _____ _____

_____ _____ _____

Taking Turns

Write the place of each child in the line.

first second third fourth fifth

1. Tina is _____ in line.

2. Chris is _____ in line.

3. Jon is _____ in line.

4. Anna is _____ in line.

5. Sam is _____ in line.

It's a Mix-Up

Read the four letters in each row.
Write the letters in order below.

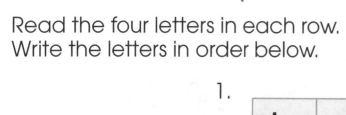

1.

h	f	i	g
f	g	h	i

2.

b	d	a	c

3.

o	m	p	n

4.

r	t	s	u

5.

y	w	x	z

6.

q	r	p	s

7.

l	j	m	k

78   Letter Sequence

Easy As ABC

Write the words in ABC order.

| ball egg dog cat apple |

1. _____

2. _____

3. _____

4. _____

5. _____

Which Is It?

Write the names of the **toys** on the **left**.
Write the names of the **animals** on the **right**.

cat ball cow top dog doll

Toys

Animals

This or That

Draw a line to the word that is opposite.

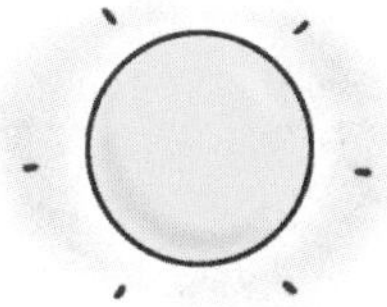

in

day

hot

old

walk

happy

night

sad

out

cold

new

run

Keep Moving

Look at the picture.
Write the correct action word.

dig walk fly run hop sleep

1. _____

2. _____

3. _____

4. _____

5. _____

6. _____

Easy Does It

Underline the sentence that goes with each picture.

1. It can run.
   It can jump.

2. It can fly.
   It can hop.

3. It can jump.
   It can dig.

4. It can hop.
   It can fly.

5. It can walk.
   It can hop.

6. It can fly.
   It can dig.

What Do You See?

Look at each picture.
Underline the correct sentence.

1. I see one.
   I see two.

2. See it go up.
   See it go down.

3. I can ride on it.
   I can jump on it.

4. I can go up.
   I can go down.

5. It can jump over.
   It can jump under.

6. It is big.
   It is little.

84   Sentence Comprehension

What Do You See?

Write the correct answer on the line.

See the ball.
1. See the dog. _____

See the doll.
2. See the ball. _____

See the dog.
3. See the boat. _____

See the doll.
4. See the boat. _____

See the cat.
5. See the doll. _____

Which Is It?

Underline the sentence that goes with each picture.

1. See the apple.
   See the toys.
   See the dog.

2. See the toys.
   See the boat.
   See the apple.

3. See the dog.
   See the apple.
   See the toys.

4. See the toys.
   See the dog and apple.
   See the toys and dog.

5. See the toys and apple.
   See the dog and apple.
   See the dog and toys.

Animal Words

Look at each picture.
Circle the word that names the picture.

1.    bed   sun   hen

2.    pet   cap   bug

3.    box   fox   ten

4.    pig   cat   dog

5.    dog   cap   cat

X Marks the Spot

Look at the pictures.
Read the story.
Then follow the directions
for the big picture.

clown   **balloon**   **dog**

The funny clown is here.
He has a funny bike.
The dog sees the funny clown.

Put an orange x on the dog.
Put a green x on the funny clown.
Put a red x on the balloon.

tree   **nest**

eggs   **bird**

The bird is by the nest.
Three eggs are in the nest.
The nest is in a tree.

Put a red x on the bird.
Put a blue x on the eggs.
Put a brown x on the nest.

What Is Wrong?

Circle the word in each row that does not rhyme.

1. **man**   **fan**   **can**   **ball**

2. **mat**   **hat**   **bow**   **bat**

3. **dog**   **log**   **hog**   **bird**

4. **boy**   **boat**   **coat**   **goat**

5. **pig**   **wig**   **hen**   **dig**

6. **run**   **shoe**   **bun**   **sun**

Things That Move

Write the word that rhymes with the underlined word.

1. I rhyme with <u>like</u>.

   _____

   - - - - - - - - - - - - - - - - - - -

   _____

2. I rhyme with <u>us</u>.

   _____

   - - - - - - - - - - - - - - - - - - -

   _____

3. I rhyme with <u>far</u>.

   _____

   - - - - - - - - - - - - - - - - - - -

   _____

4. I rhyme with <u>pet</u>.

   _____

   - - - - - - - - - - - - - - - - - - -

   _____

5. I rhyme with <u>rain</u>.

   _____

   - - - - - - - - - - - - - - - - - - -

   _____

Where Is It?

Write the correct rhyming word on the line.

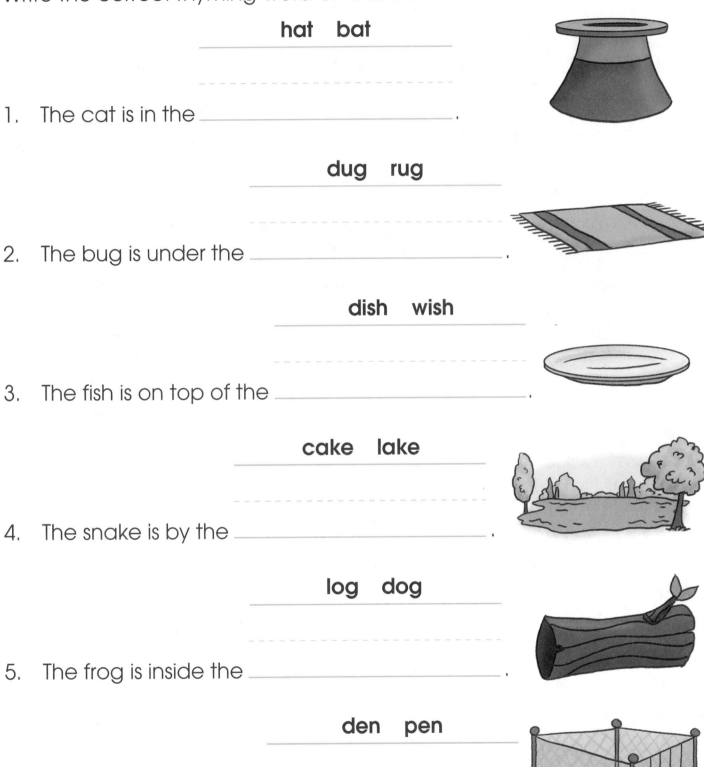

hat   bat

1. The cat is in the _____.

dug   rug

2. The bug is under the _____.

dish   wish

3. The fish is on top of the _____.

cake   lake

4. The snake is by the _____.

log   dog

5. The frog is inside the _____.

den   pen

6. The hen is outside the _____.

Same Sound

Underline the rhyming words in each sentence.

1. The king began to sing.

2. Her cat wears a hat.

3. The dog ran after the frog.

4. A vet took care of my pet.

5. My coat is in the boat.

6. I wish I had a fish.

Write It Right

Look at the picture.
Write the correct word on the line.

duck   dark

_____

1. The _____ can swim.

moon   make

_____

2. I see the _____ .

soon   sleep

_____

3. The cat likes to _____ .

hot   hat

_____

4. The dog is _____ .

bee   dig

_____

5. A _____ is on the flower.

went   wet

_____

6. My shoes are _____ .

Right or Wrong?

Look at each picture.
Were the directions followed correctly?
Circle **yes** or **no**.

1. Circle the things that we eat.

   yes **no**

2. Draw a line under animals that are pets.
   Circle the animal that lives in water.

   yes **no**

3. Cross out the pictures that rhyme.
   Circle the number.

   yes **no**

4. Draw a line under the words that begin with the letter b.
   Put an X on the zoo animal.

   yes **no**

Toss It

Cross out the one thing you **do not** need.

1. To catch fish you need:

   a fishing pole

   a boat

   worms

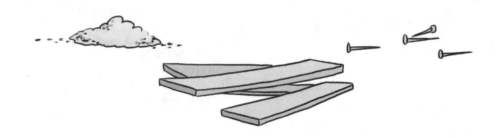

2. To make a birdhouse you need:

   wood

   nails

   bird seed

3. To cook an egg you need:

   a stove

   a pan

   a sink

4. To see a movie you need:

   money

   a hat

   a ticket

Toss It

Cross out the one thing you **do not** need.

1. To play baseball you need:

   a bat

   a hat

   a ball

2. To wash your dog you need:

   a dish

   soap

   water

3. To write a letter you need:

   a pencil

   paper

   a stamp

4. To brush your teeth you need:

   a toothbrush

   a glass

   toothpaste

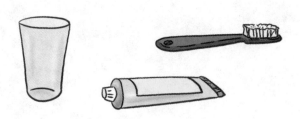

What Do You Mean?

Write the word that best completes the sentence.

large   small

1. A tiny boat is _____ .

happy   sad

2. A glad person is _____ .

slow   fast

3. Quick means _____ .

stop   begin

4. To start is to _____ .

all   some

5. Every means _____ .

A Funny Clown

Circle the correct answer.

1. The clown wears a silly hat.

   yes   **no**

2. He has a red nose.

   yes   **no**

3. He has little shoes.

   yes   **no**

4. He wears a yellow coat.

   yes   **no**

5. He has two green balls.

   yes   **no**

6. He rides a bike.

   yes   **no**

On Your Feet

Draw a line from the sentence to the correct shoes.

1. These are for snow.

2. These are for clowns.

3. These are for babies.

4. These are for running.

5. These are for puddles.

6. These are for bedtime.

Whose House?

Read the sentences.
Write each friend's name by his or her house.

1. Pedro has a flower garden.
   His house is blue.

2. Mia has a pond.
   Her house is yellow.

3. Sammy has a doghouse.
   His house is red.

Who's Who?

Read the clues.
Write each name under the correct picture.

1. Lisa rides her bike.

2. Chris likes to skate.

3. Jon likes to jog.

4. Anna walks her dog.

5. Pete likes to read.

_____

_____

_____

_____

_____

My Friends

Read the clues.
Write each name under the correct picture.

1. Sara has a green hat.

2. Mia always wears red.

3. Ken never wears blue.

4. Ty has purple shoes.

5. Mimi likes to paint.

House Call

Ben and Maisy plan to visit four friends.
Draw a line to show where they go.

First, they go to Amy's.

Next, they go to Keagan's.

Then they go to Hanna's house.

Last, they go to Peter's.

Rhyme Time

Complete each poem with a word that rhymes.

light cry me

1. Some animals hop.
    Some animals fly.
    Do some animals laugh?
    Do some animals _____?

_____

_____

2. I like to read books,
    while I'm in bed at night.
    When I get sleepy,
    I just turn out the _____ .

_____

_____

3. My dog runs after squirrels
    that climb up a tree.
    He can't reach them,
    so he runs back to _____ .

_____

_____

Seasons

Complete each poem with a word that rhymes.

1. I like the flowers growing.
   I like the birds that sing.
   I like the growing season.
   We call that season _____ .

   _____

   _____

2. I like sunny days with
   snow on the ground.
   And I like the nights
   when the moon is so _____ .

   _____

   _____

3. Some days are foggy.
   Some days are gray.
   But I like the times
   when it's sunny all _____ .

   _____

   _____

Animal Quiz

Read the clues.
Do you know what animal it is?
Write the name of the animal that matches each clue.

zebra elephant horse
raccoon wolf giraffe

1. It carries a trunk.

2. A cowboy rides one.

3. It looks like a horse with stripes.

4. It scared Little Red Riding Hood.

5. It looks like it wears a mask.

6. It has the longest neck.

Nursery Rhymes

How many nursery rhymes do you remember?
Write the name of the nursery rhyme that matches the clue.

**Mary Peter spider
Jack mouse three**

1. What ran up the clock?

_____

- - - - - - - - - - - - -

_____

2. Who had a little lamb?

_____

- - - - - - - - - - - - -

_____

3. What went up the waterspout?

_____

- - - - - - - - - - - - -

_____

4. Who eats pumpkins?

_____

- - - - - - - - - - - - -

_____

5. How many men were in a tub?

_____

- - - - - - - - - - - - -

_____

6. Who jumped over a candlestick?

_____

- - - - - - - - - - - - -

_____

Things You Know

1. Circle the things you can wear.

2. Circle the things you can eat.

3. Circle the things that are alive.

4. Circle the things you can ride.

5. Circle the things you can hear.

Barry's Dogs

Barry has two dogs.
They bark at cats.
They wag their tails.
They chew on bones.
They are his pals.

Write the correct answer.

1. How many dogs does Barry have?

   _____

   _____

2. What do they bark at?

   _____

   _____

3. What do they wag?

   _____

   _____

4. What do they chew?

   _____

   _____

5. Barry's dogs are his _____.

   _____

Jump Rope Rhyme

A-B-C-D and E-F-G
I knew that when I was three.

H-I-J-K and L-M-N-O-P
Q-R-S and T-U-V
Letters make the words I see.

W-X and Y and Z
The alphabet is fun for me!

Underline the correct answers.

1. What is the poem about?

    the sun   **the alphabet**

2. What is another good name for the poem?

    Letter Fun   **Happy Birthday**

3. What makes the words we see?

    letters   **me**

4. What is the alphabet for me?

    easy   **fun**

Question Words

Read the riddles.
Write the answers.

when	why
where	who

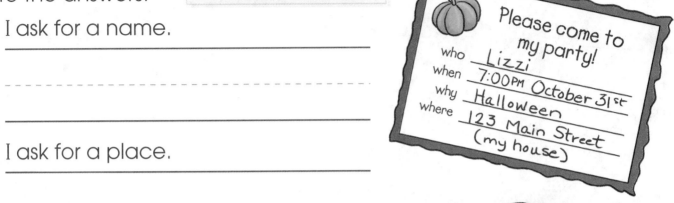

Please come to my party!

who ___Lizzi___
when ___7:00PM October 31st___
why ___Halloween___
where ___123 Main Street___
___(my house)___

1. I ask for a name.

   _____

   - - - - - - - - - - - - - - - - - - -

   _____

2. I ask for a place.

   _____

   - - - - - - - - - - - - - - - - - - -

   _____

3. I ask for a time.

   _____

   - - - - - - - - - - - - - - - - - - -

   _____

4. I ask for a reason.

   _____

   - - - - - - - - - - - - - - - - - - -

   _____

5. Write a sentence that asks what.

   _____

   - - - - - - - - - - - - - - - - - - -

   _____

   _____

   - - - - - - - - - - - - - - - - - - -

   _____

Invitation

Read the invitation.
Write the correct answer on the line.

IT'S A PARTY!

What: Dani's Birthday Party
Where: Dani's House
Date: June 4th
Time: 2:00 PM

1. Who is the party for?

_____

_____

2. What is the party for?

_____

_____

3. What time is the party?

_____

_____

4. Where is the party?

_____

_____

Erica's Note

Mom,
I went to the park.
Adam is with me. We will
be home by noon.
I love you.
Erica

Write the correct answer on the line.

1. What kind of writing is this?

    a sign   **a note**

    _____

    _____

2. Who wrote the note?

    _____

    _____

3. Who is the note to?

    _____

    _____

4. Where is Erica going?

    _____

    _____

5. Where do you like to go with a friend?

    _____

    _____

Sid the Snake

Sid the snake makes shapes.
Sid can make a circle.
Sid can make an s.
But Sid cannot make a triangle.
Sid cannot make a square.

Underline the correct answer.

1. What is the best name for the story?

    Real Snake   **Sid's Shapes**

2. What shape can Sid make?

    circle   **square**

3. Can Sid make a triangle?

    yes   **no**

4. Can Sid make an s?

    yes   **no**

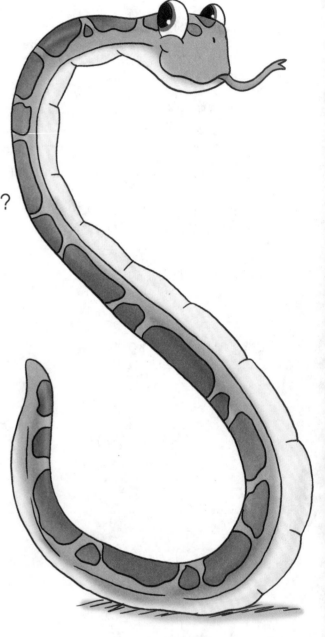

Draw a square.   **Draw a triangle.**

Where Did He Go?

Number the dog's path in order from **1** to **4**.

Toss the Penny

Get about ten pennies.
Put a muffin tin against a wall.
Stand about ten steps away.
Toss the penny into a cup.
How many pennies can you get in?

Number the sentences in
order from 1 to 4.

A. _____ Stand about ten steps away.

B. _____ Get about ten pennies.

C. _____ Toss the penny into a cup.

D. _____ Put a muffin tin against a wall.

Scary Night

The night was dark.
Tina heard something go "whooo!"
Tina was scared.
The window blew open.
Tina saw an owl.
The owl went "whooo!"
Tina was not scared then.

Number the sentences in order from 1 to 4.

A. _____ The window blew open.

B. _____ Tina saw an owl.

C. _____ Tina was scared.

D. _____ Tina was not scared then.

The Silly Man

Read the poem.

I know a silly man
who walks on his hands.
He has a silly car,
but it doesn't go far.
In his silly town,
shops are upside down.
Tell me if you can,
when you see this silly man.

Circle the correct picture.

1. Which is the silly man?

2. Which is his car?

3. Which hat would be his?

4. Which pet would be his?

Don't Be Silly

Read each sentence.
Write the correct answer.

1. Cows do not bark. What can bark?

_____

- - - - - - - - - - - - - - - - - - - -

_____

2. Cats do not fly. What can fly?

_____

- - - - - - - - - - - - - - - - - - - -

_____

3. Dogs do not lay eggs. What can lay eggs?

_____

- - - - - - - - - - - - - - - - - - - -

_____

4. Pigs do not hop. What can hop?

_____

- - - - - - - - - - - - - - - - - - - -

_____

5. Chickens do not quack. What can quack?

_____

- - - - - - - - - - - - - - - - - - - -

_____

Where Is Hero?

Look at the picture.
Read each sentence.
Where is Hero?
Draw a line to show where Hero is.

Duke is between Hero and Rags.
Rags has long fur.

Duke   Rags   Hero

The Race Is On

Read each sentence.
Color each car in the lineup.

1. The red car is last.

2. The yellow car is in the middle.

3. The blue car is behind the black car.

4. Where is the green car?

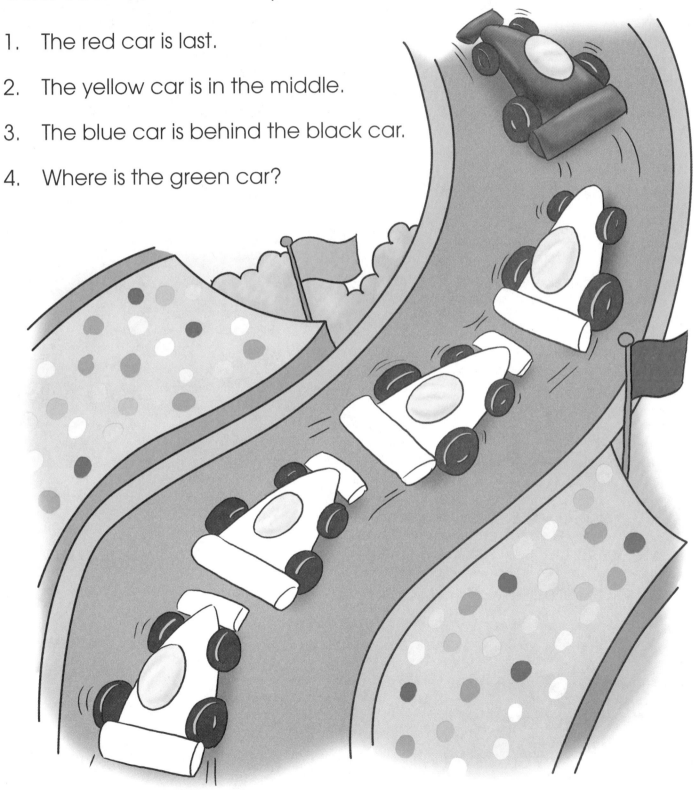

Believe It or Not

Read each pair of sentences.
Underline real or make-believe.

1. The cow jumped over the moon.   **real**   **make-believe**
   Jenny fed the cow hay.   **real**   **make-believe**

2. Puss looks for mice in the barn.   **real**   **make-believe**
   Puss came dancing out of the barn.   **real**   **make-believe**

3. An old woman lives near us.   **real**   **make-believe**
   An old woman lives in a shoe.   **real**   **make-believe**

4. Three little kittens lost their mittens.   **real**   **make-believe**
   Three little kittens were lost.   **real**   **make-believe**

What Goes with What?

Write the word that completes each sentence.

sun foot
cake bat leaves

1. is to snow as is to ____________________.

2. is to hand as is to ____________________.

3. is to ice cream as is to ____________________.

4. is to racket as is to ____________________.

5. is to rain as are to ____________________.

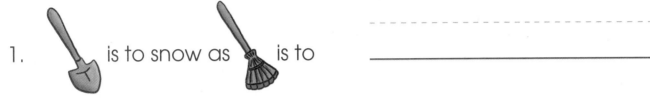

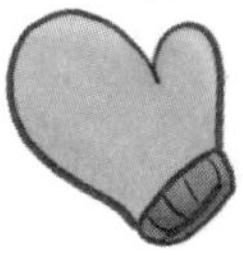

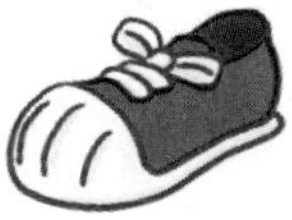

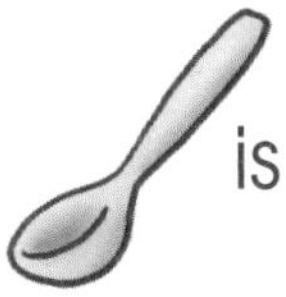

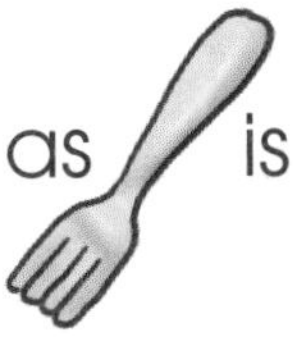

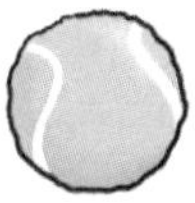

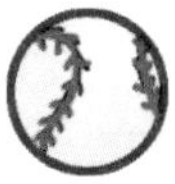

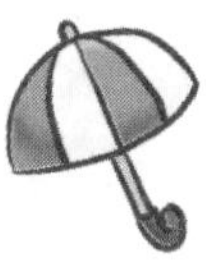

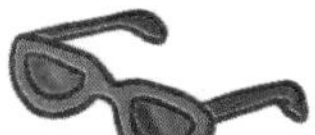

This and That

Write the word that completes each sentence.

1. is to cold as is to _____.

2. is to drink as  is to _____.

3. is to nest as is to _____.

4. is to day as is to _____.

5. is to big as is to _____.

Slippery Slide

Help Jen get down the waterslide.
Circle word pairs that rhyme.
Then draw a line to connect the word pairs.

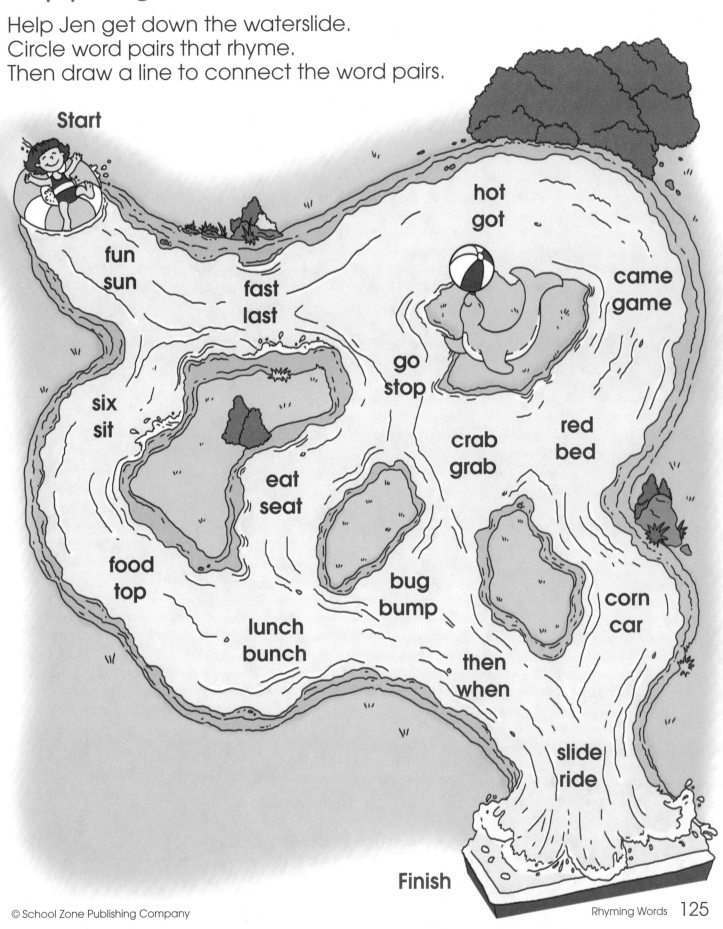

Start

fun
sun

fast
last

hot
got

came
game

six
sit

go
stop

eat
seat

crab
grab

red
bed

food
top

bug
bump

corn
car

lunch
bunch

then
when

slide
ride

Finish

Answer Key

Page 64
1. ten, cat, pig
2. bus, doll, fan
3. fish, nest, duck

Page 65
a cake, baby
e bee, leaf
i kite, tie
o boat, rope
u tube, blue

Page 66
1. fan, pie
2. rain, cat
3. hat, man

Page 67
1. leaf, tie
2. queen, dog
3. kite, ball

Page 68
1. goat, yarn
2. nine, jet
3. soap, zero

Page 69
1. pig, cup
2. web, owl
3. sun, fox

Page 70
1. drum, bed
2. bear, seal
3. book, leaf

Page 71
1. cat, cow
2. bus, dog
3. zero, bird

Page 72
1. boy, man
2. pen, sun
3. bib, pan
4. bug, ten

Page 73
1. ball   2. hat   3. pin
   fall   cat   fin
   tall   sat   win

4. can   5. wet   6. bell
   man   jet   sell
   fan   pet   tell

7. hen   8. hay   9. book
   pen   say   look
   ten   day   cook

Answers may vary.

Page 74

12 twelve

Page 75
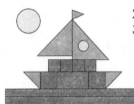

Page 76
2, 1, 3
3, 2, 1

Page 77
1. fourth
2. second
3. third
4. first
5. fifth

Page 78
1. f, g, h, i
2. a, b, c, d
3. m, n, o, p
4. r, s, t, u
5. w, x, y, z
6. p, q, r, s
7. j, k, l, m

Page 79
1. apple
2. ball
3. cat
4. dog
5. egg

Page 80
Toys	Animals
ball	cow
top	cat
doll	dog

Page 81

Page 82
1. walk
2. sleep
3. hop
4. run
5. fly
6. dig

Page 83
1. It can run.
2. It can hop.
3. It can jump.
4. It can fly.
5. It can walk.
6. It can dig.

Page 84
1. I see two.
2. See it go up.
3. I can ride on it.
4. I can go down.
5. It can jump over.
6. It is little.

Page 85
1. See the dog.
2. See the ball.
3. See the boat.
4. See the doll.
5. See the cat.

Page 86
1. See the toys.
2. See the apple.
3. See the dog.
4. See the toys and dog.
5. See the dog and apple.

Page 87
1. hen
2. bug
3. fox
4. pig
5. cat

Page 88

Page 89
1. ball
2. bow
3. bird
4. boy
5. hen
6. shoe

Page 90
1. bike
2. bus
3. car
4. jet
5. train

Page 91
1. hat
2. rug
3. dish
4. lake
5. log
6. pen

Page 92
1. king   sing
2. cat   hat
3. dog   frog
4. vet   pet
5. coat   boat
6. wish   fish

Page 93
1. duck
2. moon
3. sleep
4. hot
5. bee
6. wet

Answer Key

Page 94
1. yes
2. no
3. no
4. yes

Page 95
1. a boat
2. bird seed
3. a sink
4. a hat

Page 96
1. a hat
2. a dish
3. a stamp
4. a glass

Page 97
1. small
2. happy
3. fast
4. begin
5. all

Page 98
1. yes
2. yes
3. no
4. yes
5. no
6. no

Page 99
1. These are for snow.
2. These are for clowns.
3. These are for babies.
4. These are for running.
5. These are for puddles.
6. These are for bedtime.

Page 100

Pedro
Sammy
Mia

Page 101

 Pete
 Chris Lisa
 Anna Jon

Page 102

 Ken
Mia Ty
Mimi Sara

Page 103

Page 104
1. cry
2. light
3. me

Page 105
1. Spring
2. round
3. day

Page 106
1. elephant
2. horse
3. zebra
4. wolf
5. raccoon
6. giraffe

Page 107
1. mouse
2. Mary
3. spider
4. Peter
5. three
6. Jack

Page 108
1.
2.
3.
4.
5.

Page 109
1. two
2. cats
3. tails
4. bones
5. pals

Page 110
1. the alphabet
2. Letter Fun
3. letters
4. fun

Page 111
1. who
2. where
3. when
4. why
5. Answers will vary.

Page 112
1. Dani
2. Dani's birthday
3. 2:00 PM
4. Dani's house

Page 118
1.
2.
3.
4.

Page 113
1. a note
2. Erica
3. Erica's mom
4. the park
5. Answers will vary.

Page 114
1. Sid's Shapes
2. circle
3. no
4. yes

Page 115

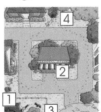

Page 116
A. 3
B. 1
C. 4
D. 2

Page 117
A. 2
B. 3
C. 1
D. 4

Page 119
1. dogs
2. birds
3. chickens
4. frogs
5. ducks

Page 120

Duke   Rags   Hero

Page 121
1. black
2. blue
3. yellow
4. green
5. red

Page 122
1. make-believe
   real
2. real
   make-believe
3. real
   make-believe
4. make-believe
   real

Page 123
1. leaves
2. foot
3. cake
4. bat
5. sun

Page 124
1. hot
2. eat
3. water
4. night
5. little

Page 125

More from School Zone

Workbooks Age-appropriate content, clear directions, and full-color illustrations make School Zone workbooks a great choice. These workbooks cover essential curriculum from preschool through sixth grade.

Card Sets Practice makes perfect! Engaging flash cards, game cards, and puzzle cards make learning lots of fun.

Start to Read!™ Books These charming books are perfect for beginning readers. Some titles come with a helpful audio CD that features the story read aloud and a number of original songs.

Boxed Software Engaging activities, friendly characters, and surprising animations provide a unique learning adventure in each skill-specific program.

Flash Action™ Software This fast-paced software transforms flash cards into interactive learning games that can be played independently or with a partner.

On-Track™ Software These award-winning electronic workbooks make the grade! The easy-to-use software provides audio guidance, tracks each child's progress, and features fun arcade games.

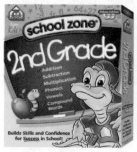

Pencil-Pal™ Software Traditional pencil-and-paper workbooks partnered with these energetic CD-ROMs offer children a variety of grade-based educational activities for hours of learning fun.

Many School Zone products are also available in bilingual editions. Visit www.schoolzone.com to learn more.

CD-ROM Warranty

Register online at www.schoolzone.com